GOD SPEAKS

A Personal Retreat with Jesus

MARK HART

Copyright © 2025 Mark Hart

All rights reserved.

Published by The Word Among Us Press
7115 Guilford Drive, Suite 100
Frederick, Maryland 21704
wau.org

29 28 27 26 25   1 2 3 4 5

ISBN: 978-1-59325-734-7
eISBN: 978-1-59325-735-4

Unless otherwise noted, Scripture texts in this work are taken from the Revised Standard Version of the Bible: Catholic Edition, copyright © 1965, 1966 National Council of the Churches of Christ in the United States of America. Used by permission. All rights reserved.

Scripture quotations marked NABRE are taken from the *New American Bible, revised edition* © 2010, 1991, 1986, 1970 Confraternity of Christian Doctrine, Washington, D.C., and are used by permission of the copyright owner. All rights reserved. No part of the New American Bible may be reproduced in any form without permission in writing from the copyright owner.

Design by Rose Audette

No part of this publication may be reproduced, stored in a retrieval system, or transmitted in any form or by any means—electronic, mechanical, photocopy, recording, or any other—except for brief quotations in printed reviews, without the prior permission of the author and publisher.
Made and printed in the United States of America

Library of Congress Control Number: 2025907421

CONTENTS

Introduction 5

1. *Encountering Jesus Unleashes God's Mercy*
Christ and the Samaritan Woman 9

2. *Encountering Jesus Unveils Your True Vocation*
Christ and Simon Peter 21

3. *Encountering Jesus Calls You Into a Relationship*
Christ and the Rich Young Man 33

4. *Encountering Jesus Invites You to Serve*
Christ and the Woman Who Washed His Feet 47

5. *Encountering Jesus Offers You Hope*
Christ and Jairus 59

6. *Encountering Jesus Unlocks Eternal Life*
Christ and Dismas 71

7. *Encountering Jesus Calls You to Greatness*
Christ and You 83

Introduction

Jesus had plenty of challenges in the years before his ministry began. For one thing, he had to make a living. Whether self-employed or as an employee, he had to work hard to make ends meet. The Gospels don't tell us what those early adult years were like for him, but I think it's safe to say that even when he was working, he was also taking time to grow in his relationship with his Father. We see that pattern—busy yet seeking time alone with the Father—later in his ministry. When I read the Gospels, it's never lost on me that Jesus was always retreating from the crowds to, well, retreat.

In short, he was taking time to grow in intimacy with the Father—time to develop a deep prayerful relationship, rooted in mutual love. Think about this: What does growing in a relationship require? One thing is for sure: it takes time. Jesus took the time, even when the crowds were pressing in upon him. We need to take the time, too, even when the busyness of life is pressing in upon us.

We need time in silence. We need time to reflect, to be present to God in our spirit—time free of stress and screens and task lists. We need times of rest.

If you're thinking, *Great, when is that supposed to happen?*, then think about what God does first thing after finishing creation: He sets apart the Sabbath, makes it holy, and commands us to keep it sacred. Why? Because "keeping holy the Sabbath" is far more than just making it to Church every Sunday for an hour. The meaning of the Sabbath runs deeper than that.

For us to truly "keep holy the Sabbath" means to enter fully—physically, emotionally, mentally, and spiritually—into communion with God. It means we rest, yes, but more to the point, we find our rest *in him.*

Unfortunately, too often Sundays have become about squeezing in Mass amid all our family responsibilities like sports tournaments, dance regionals, yard work, grocery shopping, food prep, house cleaning, paying the bills and, of course, watching football. It's not that any of these activities are flawed or bad, only that the Sabbath is meant to be so much more.

This little book is not the answer to life's busyness, but I pray it will serve as a help. Perhaps you can't get away for a couple of days for a true retreat. That's okay. The Lord has something to say to you—whether at home or away—as you draw near to him.

My prayer is that this book will help you to press "pause" on the busyness of life and hear the God of the universe speaking directly to you. Whether you reflect on each chapter on your own or with your spouse, family, or study group, I pray that the Lord's words in

INTRODUCTION

the Scripture passages we'll consider will resound in your heart in a new way.

The greatest gift you can give yourself is the gift of time with God. Once you do that, everything else in life has a tendency to fall into the right order. I hope that as you read and reflect on this little work, you'll find that the words of Jesus, our Savior, will convict your heart, challenge your mind, and fill your soul.

1

Encountering Jesus Unleashes God's Mercy

CHRIST AND THE SAMARITAN WOMAN

"He told me all that I ever did." (John 4:39)

Growing up, hide-and-seek was my favorite game. The strategy of securing the perfect hiding place, the thrill of the countdown, the heart-stopping anxiety that my six-year-old body endured, the frantic scurrying to hide and then holding my breath as I heard the seeker getting closer—it was almost too much pressure for my preadolescent heart to endure.

The lessons we learn from hide-and-seek are lessons we can carry with us throughout life: the importance of thinking under pressure, the integrity necessary to keep our eyes closed while counting, the ability to remain silent for long periods of time, and the joy derived from taking a break to play a game with friends. But the takeaways aren't just practical applications of moral development. The game offers a fundamental look at a timeless theological dilemma; namely: when it comes to God, are we really seeking him or is he the one seeking us?

FACE-TO-FACE

Too often, I treat my relationship with God like a game of hide-and-seek. At times I try to hide from him and act as though he can't see me. But of course, the problem with this thought process is: *We can't hide from God.*

To God, everything is exposed: our faults, our imperfections, and little personal secrets. But the good news is that to God, everything is also known: our talents, traits, successes, and achievements The *even better news* is that God is always seeking us: "For the Son of Man came to seek and to save the lost" (Luke 19:10). You may never miss Mass. You might read spiritual books or listen to Christian radio stations. You may wake up each day ready to earnestly seek the Lord. But the soul-stirring reality is that you're not seeking God even a fraction as much as God is seeking you.

Regardless of our sins, past or present, God constantly draws near to where we are in order to bring us to where he is.

Case in point: the Samaritan woman in St. John's Gospel. She would have been a small-town gossip's dream. She was known for her sin, and no one, certainly not a prophet or preacher, would be seen in her presence, much less engage her in a dialogue. But our Lord Jesus did precisely that. When Jesus, the Living Word, drew near, he didn't just see the sin. He saw the sinner, in need of God's mercy. In fact, the conversation between Jesus and the woman at the well is the longest recorded dialogue Jesus has with one person in any of the Gospels. Let us read those Holy Spirit-inspired words not from the perspective of a third person "reader," but as a first-person "sinner." For as the Lord sought her, he is seeking us.

> The Lord . . . left Judea and departed again to Galilee. He had to pass through Samaria. So he came to a city of Samaria, called Sychar, near the field that Jacob gave to his son Joseph. Jacob's well was there, and so Jesus, wearied as he was with his journey, sat down beside the well. It was about the sixth hour. (John 4:1, 3-6)

Why is it so important that Jesus "had to pass through Samaria" (4:1). What are we to take from this seemingly inconsequential detail?

In the time of Jesus, there was such a deep-seated hatred between Jews and Samaritans that Jews wouldn't even go into Samaria if they could avoid it. There were alternate (though far longer) routes around the region. In short, Jews would do anything avoid interacting with a Samaritan on any level.

The carpenter from Nazareth, however, was anything but politically correct. Jesus was not swayed by cultural bias or racial tension. Repeatedly, throughout the Gospels, we see our Lord shattering social norms. To put it simply, he had a divine appointment that day at the well, unbeknownst to the Samaritan woman fetching water.

St. John writes that it was "about the sixth hour" of the day (4:6), making it about high noon, the hottest part of the day. Why would she go to the well at high noon? Why not in the cooler parts of the day, like early in the morning or right before sunset?

The well was the office "water cooler" of two thousand years ago. Villagers congregated there and exchanged the best gossip before or after the day heated up. She most likely went there at noon because she had a sordid reputation and wanted to avoid the crowds who judged her. But it was at high noon—the brightest part of the day, with everything exposed and with nowhere to hide—that God came seeking.

> There came a woman of Samaria to draw water. Jesus said to her, "Give me a drink." For his disciples had gone away into the city to buy food. The Samaritan woman said to him, "How is it that you, a Jew, ask a drink of

me, a woman of Samaria?" For Jews have no dealings with Samaritans. Jesus answered her, "If you knew the gift of God, and who it is that is saying to you, 'Give me a drink,' you would have asked him, and he would have given you living water." The woman said to him, "Sir, you have nothing to draw with, and the well is deep; where do you get that living water?" (John 4:7-11)

In addition to Jews and Samaritans not mixing, men and women did not interact with one another in public, nor did they ever share a drink or a cup. Yet Jesus sat completely present to the woman, unphased by her past and deeply interested in her future. And not only did he break convention and draw near to her in public, he asked her for a drink.

Why did he do this? Because the Living Water thirsted for her salvation. The only other time we hear Jesus mention his thirst was while on the cross. In a way, this episode at the well foreshadows the cross: the thirst Jesus acknowledges here for himself foreshadows the thirst he will acknowledge on the cross for the many.

> Jesus said to her, "Every one who drinks of this water will thirst again, but whoever drinks of the water that I shall give him will never thirst; the water that I shall give him will become in him a spring of water welling up to eternal life." The woman said to him, "Sir, give me this water, that I may not thirst, nor come here to draw." (John 4:13-15)

We all experience thirst. We are born with it. It's a scientific fact that humans can go longer without food than they can go without drink. The need for spiritual drink is a matter of life and death as well.

Christ, though, is far more than a canteen for emergencies in the arid deserts of our self-involved existence. Through a midday conversation at the local watering hole, he invited this woman—and by extension, he invites us—to dive into the ocean of his mercy and experience what freedom really tastes like.

The Taste of Freedom

Jesus had a divine appointment, and he went straight to the place he wasn't supposed to go, to the person he wasn't supposed to talk with. *He wasn't revealing his thirst; he was inviting her to reveal hers!* And as he talked to her, he revealed even more.

> Jesus said to her, "Go, call your husband, and come here." The woman answered him, "I have no husband." Jesus said to her, "You are right in saying, 'I have no husband'; for you have had five husbands, and he whom you now have is not your husband; this you said truly." The woman said to him, "Sir, I perceive that you are a prophet." (John 4:16-19)

In a shocking moment ripe for reality television, Jesus revealed that not only had this woman had five husbands, . . . and she wasn't married to number six! Can you imagine how you'd feel having all your sins revealed by this seemingly random Nazorean carpenter/mystery man? All of a sudden, the Samaritan woman was face-to-face with the God of the universe—and the reality of her own shame.

To be clear, God revealed her sin not to shame her, but precisely *because* of his unfathomable love. He drew up next to her, looked her in the eye, and basically said, "I know about your shame, and I still love you." God loved her so much that he crashed into her existence, not just to forgive her, but to save her, hoping she would invite him into her life.

What would your response be if you were the one holding the bucket at that well? Would you deny the sin? Would you walk away? Or would you own your past and invite him into your life?

I Have a Confession to Make

Did you notice what happened when the woman's sin was brought into the light? We don't see her retreating in fear, but, rather, she advances for mercy. The surprising reality is that we all want truth; our hearts are hardwired for it. More to the point, everyone *needs* truth.

Some of us have convinced ourselves that we don't really have sins, but "no sin" equals "no need for a Savior." Others among us are so overwhelmed by the gravity of our past sins that we won't let God into our past. We want God to be here in our present and merciful in our future, but we hesitate to allow him into our past. We think, "You can't forgive me, Lord. I've sinned too much and I've run too far." "My sin—it's just too big." We might even lament, "Church? Oh, I can't go to church. That place will fall down if I'm in it." But the Catholic Church is a place of mercy; in fact, mercy is its mission statement! The Church counts former con artists, addicts, thieves, rapists, murderers, and heretics among the communion of saints. *Never doubt the power of God's grace or its ability to change you.*

If that's you, take a moment to tell the Lord, "I want you to walk back with me, Jesus. I trust you. Please tell me I don't have to carry this anymore. Please forgive me. Please tell me you still love me, a sinner, your child." Don't keep your past from him. Take it to Confession. You can't be made new for today or tomorrow until you invite Jesus to redeem yesterday.

When the Lord comes to you and looks you in the eye, he's not saying to you, "You are the sum of your sins and your failures." No! God's truth, to paraphrase the words of Pope St. John Paul II, is, "You are not the sum of your sins; you are the sum of the Father's love." Unless you reconcile the past, you're never going to taste the future God has designed for you.

One of the greatest things you can do for your spiritual life is to say to Jesus in prayer, "Walk with me, Lord. Walk me back into this episode, this sin, this room, this addiction, this struggle. Walk back with me and show me where you've preserved me and protected me. Reveal it to me, Lord. Pour light into my darkness. Show me where I need healing, Lord, and then please come and heal me. Come, Jesus, and save me from my darkness, my past, and myself."

The Lord reveals our shame because he loves us and wants to free us. The enemy reveals our shame because he wants to chain us and leave us there.

Samaria is half a world away, but right now, the Lord wants some face-to-face, soul-to-soul contact with you. He's saying, "You know what? Give me something to drink. I'm thirsty for your soul. I'm more thirsty for your salvation than you are; I'm more thirsty for you to know me than you are. Are you willing to lose the façade? Are you ready to let me love you?"

If you're in that place where you constantly feel pulled backward to the past, it's not time to *walk* to Confession; it's time to *run* and to experience the love of the Father. The woman at the well was made new. You have the same opportunity to be made new thanks to Christ's priesthood here on earth.

It's fascinating that in this conversation in Samaria, the woman says, "I can see you're a prophet." And then a little later, she says, "I can see you're the anointed one, the Christ." By the end of the encounter, though, she says, *"You're my Savior."* She leaves that jar of water and goes back to the town completely free—a new missionary. Unafraid and unashamed, she shares the love of Christ with those who haven't been good to her.

From Head to Heart For Reflection

1. Have there been times in your life when you've tried to hide from God? What did that look like? What were the consequences of essentially fooling yourself that God didn't see you, or worse, care about you?

2. How often do you take advantage of the Sacrament of Reconciliation? Are you frequenting the Sacrament? If not, why not?

A Step Beyond

The more grace is overflowing from you, the more others will be drawn to God themselves.

See what happened in Samaria after one sinner sipped from the chalice of God's mercy. She shared the truth with others who also came to believe:

> **Many** Samaritans from that city **believed in him because of the woman's testimony**, "He told me all that I ever did." So when the Samaritans came to him, they asked him to stay with them; and he stayed there two days. And many more believed because of his word. They said to the woman, "**It is no longer because of your words that we believe, for we have heard for ourselves, and we know that this is indeed the Savior of the world.**" (John 4:39-42, emphasis added)

God loves us even more than we love ourselves. He's also coming back at some point. That fact is only scary if we're not where we need to be in relationship to God. Open yourself to God and allow him to love you for who you truly are: a sinner in need of his mercy, an unrefined but glorious work in progress.

PRAYER

Holy Spirit, please open the eyes of my heart and reveal to me all those areas of my life where I have chosen myself instead of following you. Lord Jesus, thank you for your cross by which my sins are redeemed and the sacrament through which they are forgiven. Heavenly Father, thank you for your great and never-ending mercy even when I don't deserve it. Please give me the strength to follow you more closely. Amen.

A Personal Message from Mark Hart

2

Encountering Jesus Unveils Your True Vocation

Christ and Simon Peter

"Put out in deep water and lower your
nets for a catch." (Luke 5:4)

*F*rustration sets in. Their hands are bleeding, their forearms sore, their blood pressure rising. The boat reveals empty nets. For Simon, a husband and father, the emptiness must have struck on a deeper level. An entire night with nothing to show for it. Nights like this weren't good news for a family. As a fisherman, you can only rely so much on hard work and skill; at some point, creation (more pointedly, the Creator) needs to provide if your fishing business is to stay afloat.

Simon had obviously enjoyed success in his fishing trade with his brother Andrew. The Zebedee brothers,

James and John, were their partners, and between the two families they had two ships, and, most likely, a crew they had to pay. They had a successful operation—you don't get to that level by scraping by each day. But nights like this were worrisome.

Imagine the pressure of trying to feed your family while simultaneously lining the money purses of the tax-hungry Romans (and, by extension, the Romans' duplicitous Israelite tax collectors like Matthew). How stressful the fish-less haul must have been that night as the men worked their fingers to the bone, repeatedly casting the nets and pulling them in with nothing to show for it but sweat and growing frustration.

Then, up walks the itinerant carpenter from Nazareth, long on enigmatic charisma but short on practical angling. By the looks of Jesus, he surely doesn't strike the professional fisherman as an expert.

FACE-TO-FACE

The Holy Spirit offers us the scene through the Gospel of St. Luke.

> While the people pressed upon him to hear the word of God, . . . he saw two boats by the lake. . . . Getting into one of the boats, which was Simon's, he asked him to put out a little from the land. And he sat down and taught the people from the boat. And when he had ceased

speaking, he said to Simon, "Put out into the deep and let down your nets for a catch." And Simon answered, "Master, we toiled all night and took nothing! But at your word I will let down the nets." And when they had done this, they enclosed a great shoal of fish; and as their nets were breaking, . . . Simon Peter saw it, he fell down at Jesus' knees, saying, "Depart from me, for I am a sinful man, O Lord." (Luke 5:1-8)

Consider this scene. These are professional fishermen who tackle the unpredictable storms of Galilee at every turn. These are sailors with attitudes, tempers and, probably, "sailor language" to boot. Make no mistake, Galilee's sons are far from choir boys. Tradesmen by day, rebels by night, living under the painful and oppressive yoke of Rome season after season, catch after catch. This is the group—broken, full of pride, and tired—to whom the Lord not only draws near, but also bids to head back out on the water after the all-nighter.

Simon Peter's response offers a glimpse into the spirit of our first pope. Who can blame him for offering what seems like a less-than-affable retort to what must surely have seemed like an unreasonable request? The tone we witness from the future leader of the apostolic Church strikes me as downright annoyed and borderline condescending. "We've been at this all night, Mr. Carpenter, and you want to tell the sailors how it's done, huh?" You can almost hear the indignation in his voice. Still, what made him push away from the shore again?

Was it something in Jesus' tone that left Simon intrigued? Was it the message Jesus preached? Was it something in the Lord's glance that led Simon to stretch those tired and exhausted arms toward the oars once again? What did it take to move this weary soul into the deep after his long hard night?

How do we respond when God calls *us* out into the deep? Do we rebuff him? Do we lodge our complaint, so it's on record? Do we follow God loyally but unwillingly, perhaps out of fear of possible consequences? But does God consistently surpass, bless, shatter, and reorient our myopic and self-centered expectations? Absolutely, he does.

Our God is not lacking in creative solutions to ordinary issues. He knows what we'll say before we even pray it—yet he listens, validates, and then invites us into the deep, to rechannel our issues into effort. In the process, we gain a valuable pearl: perspective. Out in the deep, we will find that God is there with us. From that perspective we see that we're not on our own, that we haven't been abandoned in rough waters, and that all things are possible in Christ (see Philippians 4:13, Mark 9:23).

When did you last feel a storm in your heart? Maybe you felt led to leave your job but didn't have anything else lined up? Or you had to deal with *that* family member but saw it more as a burden than an opportunity? Or you were serving at your church but felt unsupported, unnoticed, or unappreciated? Or you got a call or email or text that left you feeling persecuted, abandoned, or alone? In these times, you knew God was there, but it most likely didn't feel like it.

While Sacred Scripture is clear about at least two storms on the Sea of Galilee during Christ's missionary journey, I would argue that the first account of a storm on those waters actually took place on the sea of Simon Peter's heart. The storm clouds circled, I imagine, as the fish began to leap into the tearing nets that morning. Maybe, just maybe, God was not distant but near. Was it possible that the woodworker knew as much about the fisherman as he did about the fish?

I think of Simon that day, on his knees in his slowly sinking boat weighed down with fish. His eyes were drenched with tears as a hailstorm of self-awareness rushed upon him. His ego crushed, his pride rent, his weakness revealed. His newfound awareness of his own unworthiness caused him to bid the Lord go. And yet how could this miracle worker, this rabbi, have known the hiding spot for the fish or even where these particular fishermen were, for that matter? "Depart from me," Simon said, but the Lord had no such intention.

Simon's reaction can be our first inclination as well when, as sinners, we push God away if he gets too close. *Souls trapped in darkness just cannot handle the jolting presence of such pure Light.* If we keep him at bay, we anchor him in the cove of the intellect until we realize

---

What if you, like Simon, heard the voice of the Nazorean carpenter and—out of sheer intrigue—gave him a chance at your soul?

---

that God's love is unconditional, his mercy unwavering, and, freed from the lies, we can step out in grace.

Hook, Line, and *Stinker*

Fast-forward beyond that emotional first storm in Simon's heart to the next storm we read about in Scripture, where God is sleeping (Mark 4:38) or, worse yet, not even in the boat (Matthew 14:23-33), only showing up dramatically after hours of torturous waves and loss of hope.

Perhaps you've felt it before; I know I have. You're in the thick of it—things are unraveling; the outlook is bleak, and peace is lacking. You feel like God is sleeping or, worse, doesn't care. You pray, and nothing. You cry out, and again, nada. You kneel, you scream, you beseech, you despair . . . and nothing but silence in return.

So what about *that* storm? Is it keeping you from stepping out into the deep? What if you created some space for God within your heart? What if you, like Simon, heard the voice of the Nazorean carpenter and—out of sheer intrigue—gave him a chance at your soul?

What if, after lodging your issues, complaints, and doubts, you pushed back out into the deep again? Or perhaps for the first time? What if you and I allowed the seemingly silent God to take us by the hand again? Consider the promise God gave us through the mighty prophet Isaiah:

> "I have chosen you and not cast you off,
> Fear not, for I am with you,
>> be not dismayed, for I am your God;
> I will strengthen you, I will help you,
>> I will uphold you with my victorious right hand."
>> (Isaiah 41:9-10)

If I could tattoo a verse on my brain, this would be the one: a constant reminder that God never abandons me even if I abandon him, as I sometimes do. God pursues me! He pursues you! He is the Good Shepherd, traversing valleys and mountains and riverbeds, shouting out to the lost sheep who are wandering in the valleys of torment, sin, and self-centeredness. His call evokes an urge in me to return but often leaves me feeling like I've strayed too far for the Shepherd's protection. Yet no distance, no sin, and no selfishness can separate us from the God of mercy and forgiveness.

> If God is for us, who is against us? He who did not spare his own Son but gave him up for us all, will he not also give us all things with him? Who shall bring any charge against God's elect? It is God who justifies; who is to condemn? Is it Christ Jesus, who died, yes, who was raised from the dead, who is at the right hand of God, who indeed intercedes for us? Who shall separate us from the love of Christ? Shall tribulation, or distress, or persecution, or famine, or nakedness, or peril, or sword? (Romans 8:31-35)

From Hopelessness to Hope

So what happens if we create that space in our hearts for God's life that we call grace? That little space transforms hopelessness to hope, a premise to a promise.

Why not turn to him now? Why not ask the Lord to go into the deep with you right now? Note what Jesus invites Simon to do, *after he and his crew have already been at it **their way** all night.* Get in the boat. Lift the anchor. Pick up those nets with your tired hands. Keep your grumblings to yourself. Get to work . . . but do so empowered by God's life that we call *grace*. When the mission is his and not ours, the nonstop work becomes constant privilege.

Have you accepted God's invitation to Confession yet (we spoke about this in the last chapter)? In that sacrament, Christ calls you out of your comfort zone in the midst of life's sins and storms, to rescue you and to set you free. Sometimes he extends an invitation multiple times before a heart relents. Sometimes the Spirit uses others to give us that nudge toward grace. Consider this that nudge.

From Head to Heart
For Reflection

1. When were you most aware of your own sinfulness or struggled to trust that you were worthy of the mercy God wished to offer you? Bring that time to God now in prayer.

2. Have there been times when you knew that someone was struggling and needed help, but you turned away? If so, why did you turn away? What can you do now to prepare yourself to better respond to the needs of others who are suffering through life's storms?

A STEP BEYOND

Before we can really serve God or even know God, we must come face-to-face—as Simon Peter did—with who we are and, more importantly, with who we are not. Before we can catch others in God's net, we must slow down and allow ourselves to be caught.

Christ is calling you to something more, something far greater than perhaps you have realized thus far in your life. If you want to experience the greatest joy this life has to offer, it begins with discerning what God created you for and whether you are fulfilling your mission here on earth. It begins with stepping into the deep.

While the call to follow Jesus is exciting and inspiring, serving God also means you'll be asked to give everything you have, and then some. But the rewards far exceed the demands.

Still want in? Still willing to put out into the deep of Christ, that you may be "caught"? When we put our lives in his hands, he never leaves us empty-handed. He is with us, he holds us up, and he accompanies us through all of life's storms.

Prayer

Lord, you believe in us far more than we believe in ourselves. Your plan for us is perfect and you empower us at every turn to answer our own unique calling, one that will animate every gift and blessing and talent you have entrusted to us. Holy Spirit, I give you permission this day to unleash the hidden greatness of my soul. Send me where you wish to send me and guide me all the days of my life. Amen.

A Personal Message from Mark Hart

3

Encountering Jesus Calls You Into a Relationship

Christ and the Rich Young Man

"Come, follow me." (Matthew 19:21)

Let's consider one of the most famous interactions in the Gospel narratives: the encounter between Jesus and the rich young man who went looking for heaven, only to be brought crashing down to earth.

> And behold, one came up to him, saying, "Teacher, what good deed must I do, to have eternal life?" And he said to him, "Why do you ask me about what is good? One there is who is good. If you would enter life, keep the commandments." He said to him, "Which?" And Jesus said, "You shall not kill, You shall not commit adultery, You shall not steal, You shall not bear false witness, Honor your father and mother, and, You shall love

your neighbor as yourself." The young man said to him, "All these I have observed; what do I still lack?" Jesus said to him, "If you would be perfect, go, sell what you possess and give to the poor, and you will have treasure in heaven; and come, follow me." When the young man heard this he went away sorrowful; for he had great possessions. . . . "But many that are first will be last, and the last first." (Matthew 19:16-22, 30)

FACE-TO-FACE

Oh, there Jesus goes again being illogical. The last shall be first, Jesus? In what free market economy is that true? And how is it scalable on the global stage? In what sports league, competition, or race is coming in last preferable? Who remembers the loser? How can donating my assets get me ahead on any social scale? I mean, has Jesus ever taken an economics class or a workshop on leadership?

Why would God offer freedom and salvation to the person who surrendered that which enabled him to help others? Why would God tell us the path to perfection would only come though total self-sacrifice? Easy to say such things, right? Jesus didn't have a family to feed or a mortgage to pay. The Son of Man had "nowhere to lay his head" (Matthew 8:20); the itinerant carpenter-turned-preacher didn't have monthly bills to cover. And why the stern tone with the young upstart so passionately following the moral law and desiring only to go deeper in his faith? Shouldn't this young man have been praised rather than scolded? I mean, at least this kid *was trying*!

Before we get to the meat of the verse, reread the passage above, and try to hear Christ's tone as he speaks to the passionate young truth seeker.

Does Jesus really sound upset to you? Or is something more going on? I believe he senses a genuine passion and desire in the young man. Perhaps Jesus is using this moment to redirect and unleash the fullness of that passion. Is the Lord just trying to teach *all of us* worldly souls—not just the rich young man—how deadly numbing this world can be? Is Christ inviting us to a life of material hardship or a life of spiritual freedom?

What the Lord reveals in this moment is that a relationship with him extends far beyond complying with the rules. His most ardent desire for us is rooted in relationship, not merely in rituals or rules. This is not "the rich young man versus God," but rather God reaching out to the rich young man, and, by extension, to us. Let's take it line by line.

> And behold, one came up to him, saying, "Teacher, what good deed must I do, to have eternal life?" (19:16)

Note that it was the young man who sought Jesus, not the other way around. The young man was proactively seeking truth, and Truth incarnate responded.

As we have already seen, when we seek God, he doesn't hide from us—not if we have the eyes of faith. Notice, too, that the young man addresses Christ not as "Savior" or even "Healer," but as "Teacher." Unaware of the depth and breadth of Jesus' identity, the youth views faith through the lens of an external reality—a set of dos and don'ts—rather than an internal posture that animates his faith.

> And [Jesus] said to him, "Why do you ask me about what is good? One there is who is good." (19:17)

Jesus answers a question with a question in order to initiate a deeper dialogue. This approach is the equivalent of a mental chess match, allowing the small-town carpenter to demonstrate big city wit while at the same time giving us a glimpse into the Father's heart. God is good, and in recognizing Jesus as good, as the young man surely does by approaching Jesus in the first place, the young man is plunged deeper into a reality he might not be ready or willing to grasp.

> "If you would enter life, keep the commandments." He said to him, "Which?" And Jesus said, "You shall not kill, You shall not commit adultery, You shall not steal, You shall not bear false witness, Honor your father and mother, and, You shall love your neighbor as yourself." (19:17-19)

Can merely keeping the commandments assure us of heaven? Certainly, a strict obedience to God's precepts won't hurt our chances of salvation. The letter of the law, however, can only do so much for us if we do not first adhere to the spirit of the law. In time, laws fade and obedience falters if our hearts are more concerned with the "what" of the law than the "Whom" who gave us the law out of love for us. We will not be able to stay the course. The rich young man may have never broken the speed limit, but he had no idea where he was driving or how much fuel it would take to get there. He had the directions, but his spiritual tank was running on fumes. The young man could do no more on his own. Nevertheless he offered a proud reply:

> The young man said to him, "All these I have observed; what do I still lack?" (19:20)

How fascinating that this young man, so obedient and seemingly holy, recognized in all humility that he was lacking something. What a gut check for those of us who might think we're not lacking much.

How daunting, too, is Jesus' response to this man whose holiness in action would put many of us to shame.

> Jesus said to him, "If you would be perfect, go, sell what you possess and give to the poor, and you will have treasure in heaven; and come, follow me." (19:21)

We cannot receive heaven if we are constantly clutching earth.

Let's be clear, this is not Jesus asking a middle-income earner to tithe a little more on Sundays. This is the God of the universe telling a rich man to give away *everything* and follow him and him alone. This is not only an invitation; it is a challenge and a divinely inspired secret to life: if you want it all, give it all. We cannot receive heaven if we are constantly clutching earth.

Further, when we give it all, we finally discover our true selves (see Romans 12:1). And that true self is only lived in relationship with God: "Come," Jesus says, "follow me" (Matthew 19:21).

One of the most striking lines in the passage, though, seems the most simple: Jesus instructed the rich man to give everything *to the poor*. Common sense, right? Of course he'd give it to the poor. Who needs it more? But consider what this does to the status of the rich man who is currently "above" the poor. In giving all his possessions to those "beneath" him, the rich man now relegates himself to their care. He places himself beneath those currently under him. The one who scaled the corporate ladder would not have a single rung to stand on.

This call proved too much for the young man and it is still too daunting for most of us today.

> When the young man heard this he went away sorrowful; for he had great possessions. . . . "But many that are first will be last, and the last first." (Matthew 19:22, 30)

Everlasting life, the invitation to the eternal and deepest intimacy with God, comes at a price. Discipleship will cost us everything, but it simultaneously gives us everything: We are created by God, for God. We are created for relationship.

Christ himself showed us that being in relationship is part of who we are. When he prayed the Lord's Prayer, the first line speaks of this relationship: "Our Father" (Matthew 6:9). It wasn't as if he said, "My Father." The fact that he included us when he addressed God says a lot. He told us that this is the way we ought to pray, reminding us that we are, indeed, sons and daughters of a heavenly Father, a relationship made possible by our Baptism and his cross.

Not only are you God's child, but you are also his *beloved* child. He isn't just a parent who cared *for you* (by providing food or shelter) but who cares *about you*, wanting you to share every facet of your life with him, including every fear, joy, struggle, and success. He's the Father sitting in the family room waiting for you to get home and sit with him. He is present, accessible, and interested. The love that God gives us is not distant or removed; his love is intimate, unconditional, and eternal. "Leave it all behind," he says, "and come, follow me."

How badly do you want to experience the deepest love God has to offer? How deeply do you desire life to the fullest? How far are you willing to go for God? Are you willing to open your hands and let go of all this world offers in order to experience what he promises in the next?

Jesus' challenge to the rich young man was an invitation rooted less in the surrender of the world and more in the surrender to heaven. Christ was calling him into a daily and intimate relationship, without looking back.

The rich young man was all about action. If Christ had said, "Eternal life will cost you a thousand denarii," the young man would have promptly pulled out his money bag. It would have required little, truthfully. Sure, perhaps the young man would have had to tighten his belt but, in the end, eternal life wouldn't have really required his heart.

In essence, Jesus was saying that eternal life would cost the rich young man a thousand denarii, paid out one coin at a time, one day at a time, for the rest of this life. The cost of eternal life is ongoing discipleship, constant conversion of heart, and reckless abandon to the will of the Father.

Do you still desire it? What earthly pleasures do you grasp? What counterfeit heavens and personal luxuries keep you from turning that corner in your faith life?

Choose Life

Do you want to live a life of abundance, allowing the Father to love you, Christ to forgive you, and the Holy Spirit to dwell in you? That kind of life is in your hands. In the smallest of ways, many barely noticeable, your life makes a difference every minute of every day, for better or for worse. The world is an ongoing play in which you have an essential role, even if you don't see it. Each moment, the Lord is setting a choice before you, to follow him and bring life or to reject his truth and, in some measure, bring death. He's asking you, directly, "Do you want to abide in me? Will you remain in me? Do you desire to live in me and allow me to dwell within you?" These are questions everyone must ask themselves, and these are choices that everyone must make.

> I call heaven and earth to witness against you this day, that I have set before you life and death, blessing and curse; therefore choose life, that you and your descendants may live, loving the LORD your God, obeying his voice, and cleaving to him; for that means life to you and length of days. (Deuteronomy 30:19-20)

Many take the easy path, and why not? It's always easier not to sacrifice, not to forgive, not to love, . . . but "easy" isn't the gospel! The road to heaven is arduous and steep; the road to hell is paved with earthly gold and even has an HOV lane. But, "I have set before you life and death; . . . choose life, that you and your descendants may live." Those words from Deuteronomy were written well over three thousand years ago, and they are as true in the twenty-first century as they were then. God's wisdom is good that way; it's both timeless and timely.

God, in his divine mercy, sets before us choices each day that offer us the opportunity to build up or to tear down, to bring life or to destroy it. God invites us to pray, "Thy Kingdom come," as a reminder that my own kingdom—the false kingdom of self-interest before concern for others—must go. What mark on the world will your life leave this day? The answer, quite literally, is in your hands. Choose life.

From Head to Heart
For Reflection

1. The rich young man had the humility to recognize that something was lacking in his life. What about you? Consider those areas of your life where greater humility could help you grow in abandonment to God and love for your neighbor.

2. What choices have you made recently that drew you closer to God? What choices drew you away from God? In each instance, reflect on why you made your choices and how you can strengthen the good and eliminate the bad so that in every instance you are choosing life.

A Step Beyond

Review your daily and weekly schedule. Look through your calendar, appointments, activities, and responsibilities. Next, review your smartphone, emails, social media posts and consumption, and your monthly bank statement.

Who and what have become priorities in your life? Where do your time and your treasure go? What monopolizes your attention? Where has earth taken precedence over heaven and diverted your eyes from upward to downward to inward?

Identify any false gods that have taken over your life. Name them and then have the courage to prayerfully let them go. We cannot taste heaven if we are constantly clutching the hems and robes of false gods.

Clasped and closed hands signal death. Open hands usher in life.

Choose wisely.

PRAYER

Lord God, your most fervent desire is to have a deep, abiding, and eternal relationship with me. Too often, I have taken my eyes off of the heavenly and sought the things of earth. Help me to see more clearly those things or people or places that sometimes obstruct my hope of heaven. Identify for me and convict me of where I may be seeking false gods instead of you, the one true God. Be the Lord of my life and my sole pursuit in this world until you call me home to heaven. Amen.

A Personal Message from Mark Hart

4

Encountering Jesus Invites You to Serve

CHRIST AND THE WOMAN WHO WASHED HIS FEET

"Wherever this gospel is preached in the whole world, what she has done will be told in memory of her."
(Matthew 26:13)

Do you remember the story of Sts. Martha and Mary? Of course you do. Every Christian has heard at least one homily praising Mary who sat at the Lord's feet while her sister Martha (patron saint of waiters and waitresses, true story) scurries around waiting on Jesus. For Martha, doing is always easier (and often preferable) to being.

FACE-TO-FACE

Let's take a look:

> Now as they went on their way, he entered a village; and a woman named Martha received him into her house. And she had a sister called Mary, who sat at the Lord's feet and listened to his teaching. But Martha was distracted with much serving; and she went to him and said, "Lord, do you not care that my sister has left me to serve alone? Tell her then to help me." But the Lord answered her, "Martha, Martha, you are anxious and troubled about many things; one thing is needful. Mary has chosen the good portion, which shall not be taken away from her." (Luke 10:38-42)

Martha usually gets a pretty bad rap. Consider what the story tells us: she was serving the Lord. Apparently, Martha's "love language" was acts of service. Moreover, hospitality is foundational in Mediterranean culture. To serve another is a way of honoring them, your people, your culture, and your God. If anything, one would think that Christ would give *Mary* the eye roll. Yet Jesus corrects . . . *Martha?*

Shakespeare offered "To be or not to be?" as an important question. In this scene, however, the Lord seems to offer an alternate question: "Is it better to *be* or to *do?*"

For many of us, it's far easier to show love through tasks than through the complete and utter emotional presence of simply being with another. We really are a culture of human *doings* and not human *beings*.

Unfortunately, this attitude bleeds into our prayer life: It's far easier to love others in the name of Christ by *doing* than it is to just sit and *be* with Christ in our daily prayer time. We replace our prayer with projects, our contemplation with completed tasks, and we wonder, "Where is God?"

As Venerable Fulton Sheen reminded us, "Ever since the days of Adam, man has been hiding from God and saying, 'God is hard to find.'" Sometimes we just get too busy to notice the God of the universe right before us.

The exact opposite is true of Christ. He is constantly present and ever available to us. He is waiting and desiring the most intimate relationship possible with each and every one of us.

During his visit to Australia for World Youth Day in 2008, Pope Benedict XVI developed this concept that we must first "be" (receive Christ) before we can "do" (offer Christ):

> These gifts of the Spirit . . . are neither prizes nor rewards. They are freely given (cf. 1 Cor 12:11). And they require only one response on the part of the receiver: I accept! **Here we sense something of the deep mystery of being Christian. What constitutes our faith is not primarily what we do but what we receive.**

After all, many generous people who are not Christian may well achieve far more than we do. Friends, do you accept being drawn into God's Trinitarian life? . . . into his communion of love? (Vigil with the Young People, July 19, 2008, emphasis added)

Do you see what he said there? He is not just saying, "You can't give what you don't have." In essence, he's saying, "It's better to receive than to give," or, more to the point, "To be a Christian, we must first receive Christ and the gifts of the Spirit." Then, and only then, can we give to others, can we be doers.

Anyone can serve the poor, including atheists who might be far more active in this regard than many Christians. Christians, however, though equally as moved by the desire to relieve suffering, are motivated and empowered by a different "why" and "who." The gospel call to serve the poor is our "why," and God, through the saving work of Jesus and the power of the Holy Spirit, is our "who." If we show up to serve at our parish or in our community but we haven't prayed about why, we're not glorifying the Holy Trinity as much as we are praising the minor "trinity": me, myself, and I.

In short, our acts of service (our doing) should flow from our times of prayer (our being).

It is with this understanding that we turn attention to our next Scripture story, set at yet another dinner party, when an unexpected guest demonstrates what true holiness looks like.

A Jar-ring Scene

> Now when Jesus was at Bethany in the house of Simon the leper, a woman came up to him with an alabaster jar of very expensive ointment, and she poured it on his head, as he sat at table. But when the disciples saw it, they were indignant, saying, "Why this waste? For this ointment might have been sold for a large sum, and given to the poor." But Jesus, aware of this, said to them, "Why do you trouble the woman? For she has done a beautiful thing to me. For you always have the poor with you, but you will not always have me. In pouring this ointment on my body she has done it to prepare me for burial. Truly, I say to you, wherever this gospel is preached in the whole world, what she has done will be told in memory of her." (Matthew 26:6-13)

It's a beautiful story, is it not? An unnamed woman crashes the dinner party to anoint and bathe the Lord's feet. This is the kind of scene that reality TV often contrives—raw human emotion free of social decorum.

Even more fascinating, though, is the identity of this woman as revealed by St. John, Jesus' closest disciple, in a parallel story:

> Six days before the Passover, Jesus came to Bethany, where Lazarus was, whom Jesus had raised from the dead. There they made him a supper; Martha served, and Lazarus was one of those at table with him. Mary took

Our *doing* must flow forth from our *being*, as it did with Mary of Bethany who sat at the feet of Jesus.

a pound of costly ointment of pure nard and anointed the feet of Jesus and wiped his feet with her hair; and the house was filled with the fragrance of the ointment. But Judas Iscariot, one of his disciples (he who was to betray him), said, "Why was this ointment not sold for three hundred denarii and given to the poor?" This he said, not that he cared for the poor but because he was a thief, and as he had the money box he used to take what was put into it. Jesus said, "Let her alone, let her keep it for the day of my burial. The poor you always have with you, but you do not always have me." (John 12:1-8)

While the Gospel accounts vary on certain details and some scholars may disagree, it is more than plausible that the woman who anointed Christ prior to his own death was none other than Mary of Bethany, the sister of Martha and Lazarus.

This detail is important to our purposes here because, as Pope Benedict XVI reminded us, it is only *after we receive* that we can rightly *give*. It is only after we have received the mercy, grace, and presence of God that we are empowered to serve in his name. In short, our *doing* must flow forth from our *being*, as it did with Mary of Bethany who sat at the feet of Jesus.

For this reason, Mother Teresa of Calcutta insisted that her Missionaries of Charity spend a full hour in Adoration of the Blessed Sacrament (the Eucharist) every single morning *prior* to serving the poor. Did the poor not have needs during those sixty minutes?

Of course they did. Would it not have been a beautiful, merciful act to feed them for an additional sixty minutes? Sure. What Mother Teresa understood, however, was that if the service did not flow from the altar of mercy, eventually that river of mercy would cease to flow.

You have nothing to give but Christ in you. Everything else you offer will, in time, break, fade, distract, or die. We have nothing eternal to offer except the presence of Christ within us. We are empowered to make that offering through the Holy Spirit whom Pope Benedict has called "the soul of our soul." Everything else is fleeting; Christ alone is eternal.

And Yet

And yet too often we're more comfortable serving the food than adoring the Lord. Truthfully, sometimes it appears more noble to do so. Serving others all night? Yes, I'm comfortable with that. But publicly adoring the one true God of the universe with every fiber of my being? And being so moved that I wash his feet? Let's not get fanatical here, right? Put the cork back in the alabaster jar.Consider what Jesus said after he washed the feet of his disciples:

> "I have given you an example, that you also should do as I have done to you." (John 13:15)

Jesus could not put it more simply. Here he gives us a window into the Father's heart. He's saying, "I give my everything—all of myself—every single time. I hold nothing back, and nor should you." A day later, on the cross, he put the exclamation point to this very fact.

God the Father, our Creator, knows what we're capable of. He wants us to realize and become all that we can be through the power of the Holy Spirit, not just to settle for all that we currently are. How do we get to that place? By receiving the Lord in daily prayer.

As the great French novelist and poet Léon Bloy once penned, "The only real sadness, the only real failure, the only great tragedy in life, is not to become a saint." God gives you the grace necessary to become a saint as you sit with him in prayer and then "do" with him in service. Sts. Martha and Mary offer us invaluable insight into such discipleship. To serve the Lord is a high privilege, but to adore the Lord is the highest praise.

St. Mary of Bethany came face-to-face with God, she experienced his mercy, and she allowed it to fuel her every action and desire, regardless of public perception, scorn, or judgment.

Mary sets the bar high, challenging each of us to do the same.

From Head to Heart For Reflection

1. Do you have a daily prayer time? Are you able to stick with it? If not, consider when and where you try to accomplish this essential task. Does it need to be earlier? Later? In a quieter place? Away from the computer? Do you use Scripture? Even if everything is running smoothly, review the logistics of that time to see how you can bring the most to your daily prayer time and receive the most from it.

2. How comfortable are you just letting yourself be in the presence of God? If this is a challenge—and it is for all of us at least some of the time—ask him to help you calm your spirit. Set a timer, if that will help, and sit in his presence for five minutes, allowing him to be present to you. Gradually increase that time until you are able to rest in his presence, praising him and listening for his word to you.

3. Identify those areas in your life where you can be slothful (spiritually lazy). What are some ways you can let the Holy Spirit unleash new layers of greatness from within you? Write them out. Share them with people you know and whom you trust will hold you accountable.

A Step Beyond

Raise your spiritual bar and keep it high. When you do, know this: you are actually helping others grow closer to Christ. God can do more with your example than you can imagine. Embrace humility. Seek holiness. Seek the quiet presence of God. Then smash the alabaster jar and hold nothing back. God deserves your best effort—all that you are—every single day. If you woke up with air in your lungs, it is a sure sign he's not done with you yet. Give your best to God, daily, because he deserves it.

Prayer

Heavenly Father, you call us to serve others out of our love for You. Reveal to me all those times that I put actions or tasks ahead of my prayer time with you. Help me to identify those common "traps" that seek to distract me from adoring you, hearing your voice, or seeking silent quality time with you first and foremost. Please put a burden on my heart to spend time with you daily and to seek you throughout the entirety of my day from when I wake until I sleep. Amen.

A Personal Message from Mark Hart

5

Encountering Jesus Offers You Hope

CHRIST AND JAIRUS

"Do not fear, only believe." (Mark 5:36)

"He will need to be restrained for this," the nurse explained to my wife and me. Just one week after the birth of our son, we were back in the hospital with him as, writhing in pain, he fought a serious infection. Standing there draped in lead jackets for my protection, I was now holding down my wailing baby boy as he was strapped to a board and slowly moved into an imaging machine. Hopeful yet helpless, my wife and I found that our love for this tiny soul reached new levels. It's astounding how painful it can be to watch another—especially a little one—suffer.

As a father, I would have given anything, *anything*, to trade places with him. The world has it wrong when it says, "If God were *truly good* there wouldn't be any more suffering." That day gave me new appreciation for the cross, and new insight into our heavenly Father. We focus on Christ's sacrifice on Good Friday—and rightly so—but how often to we focus on the sacrifice of the Father, giving his only Son, perfect and blameless, as a ransom for the rest of his children? I caught a glimpse of God the Father's love for us in the midst of my own tears and suffering. Suffering reveals not the absence of love, but the depths of it.

Perhaps you, like me, have held an anxious mother in that gut-wrenching moment when the ultrasound shows that the heartbeat has stopped. Maybe you, too, have sat bedside with that loved one in hospice care, clinging to sacred moments where life is thrust into perspective as one soul passes from here to eternal life. Maybe you have also held a child who's experienced bullying or comforted a friend suffering through a divorce. It's in moments like these that our humanity really comes into focus, doesn't it? It's in these moments when life slows to a pause that we taste our own mortality. We come face-to-face with who we *really are*, who God designed us to be, and the point of life.

FACE-TO-FACE

One of the most poignant and touching biblical scenes for me has always been the story of the synagogue official, Jairus, who draws near to Jesus seeking healing for his daughter who is near death.

> And when Jesus had crossed again in the boat to the other side, a great crowd gathered about him; and he was beside the sea. Then came one of the rulers of the synagogue, Jairus by name; and seeing him, he fell at his feet, and besought him, saying, "My little daughter is at the point of death. Come and lay your hands on her, so that she may be made well, and live." And he went with him.
>
> And a great crowd followed him and thronged about him. . . . While he was still speaking, there came from the ruler's house some who said, "Your daughter is dead. Why trouble the Teacher any further?" But ignoring what they said, Jesus said to the ruler of the synagogue, "Do not fear, only believe." And he allowed no one to follow him except Peter and James and John the brother of James. When they came to the house of the ruler of the synagogue, he saw a tumult, and people weeping and wailing loudly. And when he had entered, he said to them, "Why do you make a tumult and weep? The child is not dead but sleeping." And they laughed at him. But he put them all outside, and took the child's father and mother and those who were with him, and

went in where the child was. Taking her by the hand he said to her, "Talitha cumi"; which means, "Little girl, I say to you, arise." And immediately the girl got up and walked; for she was twelve years old. And immediately they were overcome with amazement. And he strictly charged them that no one should know this, and told them to give her something to eat. (Mark 5:21-24, 35-43)

When the synagogue official, Jairus, falls at the feet of Jesus, he is looking for a miracle. He heads to the carpenter and asks the Divine Physician to make a house call. Earth cried out to heaven, and heaven responded.

Note, however, that while Christ immediately headed out to the official's home, an unexpected turn of events delayed his response. We would be wise to realize—especially when asking for healing from God—that the timetable is his, not ours. God healed on his timetable, not Jairus'. What sidetracked Jesus on his direct path to the house of Jairus? The healing of the woman with a hemorrhage who crept up and touched the hem of his garment (see 5:25-34).

Imagine how Jairus must have felt in that moment when the woman's healing interrupted Jesus' travel. Time was of the essence. Jairus had one plan; God had another. Jairus wanted God to act immediately; God acted eventually.

God's timing rarely matches ours, and with good reason. God is timeless and we are not. Think about that fact for a moment. Did God respond? Yes, initially.

Was it the way Jairus would have liked? No. But was God still faithful? Absolutely.

Let's break this passage down into smaller pieces so as not to miss any details the Holy Spirit is offering us. After each Gospel line, contemplate this rich scene in light of your own faith walk.

> Then came one of the rulers of the synagogue, Jairus by name; and seeing him, he fell at his feet. (5:22)

Do you believe that God knows your name? That God calls you by name and, even, has your name "graven . . . on the palms" of his hands" (Isaiah 49:16), promising he will never forget you?

> Jairus . . . besought him, saying, "My little daughter is at the point of death. Come and lay your hands on her, so that she may be made well, and live." And he went with him. And a great crowd followed him and thronged about him. (5:22, 23-24)

To "beseech" is more than to ask, it's to implore with urgency and with fervor. Do you beseech God? Do you go to him with urgency and fervor when you pray for others?

> While he was still speaking, there came from the ruler's

house some who said, "Your daughter is dead. Why trouble the Teacher any further?'" (5:35)

Do you trust in the Lord's timing? Do you trust in his plan more than your own?

But ignoring what they said, Jesus said to the ruler of the synagogue, "Do not fear, only believe." (5:36)

Did you notice that the Lord posits "belief" (faith) as the antithesis and antidote to fear in this scene? Why do you think that is?

And he allowed no one to follow him except Peter and James and John the brother of James. When they came to the house of the ruler of the synagogue, he saw a tumult, and people weeping and wailing loudly. (5:37-38)

Why were only Jesus' closest followers allowed to come with him? Do you think they more capable of handling the situation than the others?

And when he had entered, he said to them, "Why do you make a tumult and weep? The child is not dead but sleeping." And they laughed at him. But he put them all outside, and took the child's father and mother and those who were with him, and went in where the child was. (5:39-40)

Have you or anyone you know ever mockingly laughed at God? Have you ever given up on a person, a situation, or a problem only to have God reduce your smugness to ashes and crush your pride into dust?

> Taking her by the hand he said to her, "Talitha cumi;" which means, "Little girl, I say to you, arise." And immediately the girl got up and walked; for she was twelve years old. And immediately they were overcome with amazement. (5:41-42)

How long did it take God's grace to restore the girl to new life? Why is the adverb "immediately," used twice, so vital to the scene?

> And he strictly charged them that no one should know this, and told them to give her something to eat. (5:43)

Why do you think Jesus ordered them to be silent about what he had done?

Take a moment and put yourself in that bedroom in Jairus' house. Which character are you? Are you one of the apostles, looking in wonder at the Rabbi after what he just did? Are you, possibly, Jairus or his wife, wiping away tears of gratitude as you stare into the eyes of mercy? Or are you the daughter, coming to consciousness as you would from a long and deep sleep, the Lord's face slowly coming into focus as you rise?

Peer into Jesus' eyes and know that whatever vantage point you take, whatever character you identify with, the Lord's gaze, as you look in his eyes, is focused solely on you. Just so, he is always looking upon us, watching over us, and inviting us to trust him more perfectly.

Prayer, Hope, and God's Plan

Too often we put the Timeless One on our own timeline, don't we? Had Jesus made it to Jairus' home while his daughter was ailing but still alive, would the miracle have been as impressive to those present or to those of us reading about it so many centuries later? Would Jairus and his wife have been as grateful or as devoted to the Lord if he'd merely healed a fever and not raised their preteen from the dead? I was assuredly more grateful to the doctors in the neonatal intensive care unit for helping my son through a potentially fatal illness than I would be for the doctor who listens to a cough and prescribes medicine. Sure, both are helping, but the context affects my level of gratitude—and, perhaps, my prayer response.

Often we hit our knees in prayer most fervently when we are out of options. Jesus becomes our last resort when everything else we try fails. Now, to be clear, God welcomes these prayers as he does all prayers. But suffering offers us not only the gift of patience, but also the gift of dependence. God wants to be the forethought *and* the afterthought. It is when we are suffering the most, when we begin to buckle under the weight of the stress or fear or pain, that prayer is where the cross changes shoulders.

While God does not will our suffering, he can allow it: "In your hearts reverence Christ as Lord. Always be prepared to make a defense to any one who calls you to account for the *hope* that is in you" (1 Peter 3:15, emphasis added).

There's a famous saying that to be successful one must "begin with the end in mind." If that is the case, there is no better example of "success" than what we find in the Gospels. God, from the beginning, had a detailed plan to save us through the birth, death, and resurrection of Jesus.

For this reason, we say that Jesus was "born to die." When God emptied himself and took flesh (see Philippians 2:7), he was on a mission. Christ came to do for us what we could not do for ourselves. In both of these events—his birth and his death—history and the future were changed forever, and hope found an unshakable foundation.

From Head to Heart For Reflection

1. Do you invite Christ into your suffering as a last resort or as a first response? How might sharing your burden with him in prayer strengthen your ability to endure?

2. Do you trust Jesus when he tells you not to fear? "Do not fear" happens to be the most oft-spoken command in the Bible. Why do you think that is?

3. Think of a time you have endured a particularly challenging trial. In retrospect, what enabled you to endure? Did you find yourself growing in patience or hope? If so, why? If not, why not?

A Step Beyond

It's easy to allow our prayer to become all about us, but when we do that, we miss out on an amazing opportunity to draw closer to the mystical body of Christ—to those around us or those who have gone before us.

Open your journal or a new document on your computer and list everyone in your life who needs prayer. Begin with those closest to you, but then include the souls you've encountered whom you hardly know but whom the Spirit tapped you on the shoulder when you interacted with them. It could be the grumpy teller at the bank, the stressed-out barista at the coffee shop, or the clerk who shared her life story with you as she checked out your groceries.

Rather than petitioning God on behalf of your own intentions, take that list and all of those souls to prayer, asking God to bless them and their intentions. Look to God with an expectant heart and wonder. Look to Christ with hope and gratitude as Jairus and his wife did and as his three apostles did. Allow the Spirit to open your eyes to the power of Jesus as he did for that risen child so many centuries ago. And allow the Spirit to bring you to a firmer hope in the One who saves you and cares for you, day in and day out.

PRAYER

Lord Jesus, you know more than anyone what it means to suffer, yet you never abandoned your trust in nor your love for the Father. Lord, increase my faith in times of suffering and seasons of turmoil. Send your Spirit of consolation to be with me and to increase my trust in you and in your perfect and providential plans. Thank you for the gift of your cross, your suffering, your death, and your resurrection. Help me to never lose hope. I do believe, Lord, but please "help my unbelief." Amen.

A Personal Message from Mark Hart

6

Encountering Jesus Unlocks Eternal Life

CHRIST AND DISMAS

"Jesus, remember me when you come into your kingdom." (Luke 23:42, NABRE)

One evening, while the local news was on the television, the weather report came on. Living in Arizona, meteorology is not an exact science, nor is it exactly fortune-telling. There are only so many ways to say, "It's going to be hotter than Gehenna." This particular night, the broadcast got our attention because the forecast called for the chance of rain. During the report, the meteorologist said that the following day would be partly cloudy but the weekend would be mostly sunny. The distinction prompted an interesting question from my then seven-year-old: "Daddy, what's the difference between partly cloudy and mostly sunny?"

Wanting to avoid a dialogue in which I revealed my ignorance while bellowing on about cloud density and barometric pressure, I opted for a simpler response: "Well, sweetie, I guess it depends whether the weatherman is an optimist or a pessimist."

I go back to that moment every time I hear one or the other used in a weather report. We're reminded in Scripture that God "sends rain on the just and on the unjust" (Matthew 5:45). We will all have good days and bad days—sunny days and days filled with life's storms. But, as Fulton Sheen said, "The major difference in human beings is not in what happens to them, but in how they react to what happens."

FACE-TO-FACE

Scripture tells us about "the good thief" that tradition names as Dismas, the one who beseeches mercy from Mercy in the waning hours of Good Friday. We know the episode well: one thief bad, and the other good. This beautiful episode appears only in St. Luke's Gospel, yet it gives us invaluable insight into both God and Good Friday. St. Luke's insight becomes clearer, however, when we begin with St. Matthew's account of the crucifixion.

> Then two robbers were crucified with him, one on the right and one on the left. And those who passed by

> derided him, wagging their heads and saying, "You who would destroy the temple and build it in three days, save yourself! If you are the Son of God, come down from the cross." So also the chief priests, with the scribes and elders, mocked him.... And *the robbers who were crucified with him also reviled him in the same way.* (Matthew 27:38-41, 44, emphasis added)

Note that when the crucifixions began, both criminals crucified with him joined in the mockery. There was no "good thief" when the day began, at least not that we saw. The souls on the right and left of the cross saw only condemnation hanging between them. Jesus was obviously no one special, for no true god would allow himself to be butchered and destroyed as this rabbi had been. No one capable of stopping this level of brutality and abuse would endure such pain.

So what changed in the heart of Dismas that afternoon? What happened during those three hours? What did he witness of the One hailed as "King of the Jews" as he suffered beside him? What inspired this bad thief to turn good on this Good Friday?

> One of the criminals hanging there reviled Jesus, saying, "Are you not the Messiah? Save yourself and us." The other, however, rebuking him, said in reply, "Have you no fear of God, for you are subject to the same condemnation? And indeed, we have been condemned justly, for the sentence we received corresponds to our

crimes, but this man has done nothing criminal." Then he said, "Jesus, remember me when you come into your kingdom." He replied to him, "Amen, I say to you, today you will be with me in Paradise." (Luke 23:39-43, NABRE)

Perhaps it was the gentleness in Jesus' tortured spirit. It may have been the charity in his labored words between gasping breaths. Maybe it was compassion in the sideward glance through bruised, barely open eyes. Whatever it was, it made an impact on Dismas. Hanging in the presence of innocence, his own guilt became all the more clear. As the sky grew dark, the Light shone more brightly. The convict was now convicted that the man in the middle had indeed done nothing wrong.

The revelation is even more illuminating in the dialogue between the left and the right. The criminal on the left begins calling Christ out, almost demanding him to act. His cries are out of self-interest, though, not out of self-condemnation or adoration. "Save yourself, and us!" is the cry of a soul who wants the pain to stop and the sentence reversed. "We are receiving our due reward of our deeds," however, is the cry of a penitent soul who accepts the pain. "Remember me" is a soul begging to have the sentence not reversed but redeemed. As Fulton Sheen so eloquently put it, "The thief on the left wanted to be taken down but the thief on the right wanted to be taken *up*."

Making Sense Out of Suffering

So why do many today find suffering and, by extension, Jesus himself, suffering for us on the cross, impossible to reconcile with modern culture? I think it's largely because the modern world cannot stand what it cannot explain or control. Modern culture cannot fathom how humanity can land a probe on Mars but not solve the problem of suffering. Sure, we can counsel it, medicate it, run from it, or try to ignore it, but in the end none of those remedies or distractions act as solutions to the problem of suffering. Suffering only makes sense in Christ.

We get a deeper glimpse into the meaning of the suffering of Jesus himself when we read of the moment the soldier pierces his side with a lance (see John 19:34). As Scripture notes, when Christ died, blood and water flowed from his side. This signals the conception of his Church with the blood and waters of God's divine mercy. It's in the midst of the blood and water, though, that we see where the thief on the left went wrong and where Dismas got it right.

The bad thief wanted the suffering to end but showed no penitence or desire to change. "Get me out of this!" was his plea. Many of us go to God in moments of desperation, looking for relief; but once the suffering is over, go back to our own devices. It's as if we're saying, "I want the healing but not the accountability. I'll take

Baptism is precisely that—a *death* to this world but with the promise of the next. We cannot expect the crown without the thorns, nor the reward without the risk.

your blood if it will make my bleeding stop, . . . but you can keep the water of Baptism that would call me out of my own way of life."

Others in life prefer the water of Baptism but not the blood of sacrifice. They want to be part of "the Jesus club"—to be included as his children and have assurance of salvation. They want the glory of heaven on an earthy throne.

The same instinct seems to be at work when James and John of Zebedee approach the Lord, asking him "to do for us whatever we ask of you . . . to sit, one at your right hand and one at your left, in your glory" (Mark 10:35, 37). It wasn't good enough for James and John to be counted among the twelve, they wanted preferential treatment; they wanted to be #1 and #1A on the VIP list. At the time, they still misunderstood the purpose of Christ's mission, which kingdom they were seeking, and the path it took to get there.

The glory of heaven doesn't come without tasting death on earth: death to sin, death to pride, death to self. This is why Baptism is so vital, so primary and so life-altering. This is why we are baptized not only into Jesus' life but also into the Lord's death. Baptism is precisely that—a *death* to this world but with the promise of the next. We cannot expect the crown without the thorns, nor the reward without the risk.

And yet sometimes, I'm like the thief on the left. I want Jesus to take away my pain, take away my bitterness, take away my anger, my temptations, my fears, loneliness, and all those other frustrations. "Take them away God. You can heal me, but I'm not looking for you to save me."

I don't know why we fear going to Christ as Savior. When we do, when we come to him as penitent—in need of a savior—he always meets us with compassion. Just look at his overwhelming love for Dismas on the cross. Sure, the game changes, for now we will be expected to act and live differently, but it changes in the best way possible: ultimately, as Dismas learned, we will be with him in paradise.

As we embrace the water of Baptism *and* the blood of sacrifice, the joys *and* the sufferings, grace can take effect and do what it is designed to do: bring life.

Never Forget

The plea of Dismas—"remember me"—presents us with a fascinating word: *remember*. In our Western culture we use it in a variety of ways: to recall a relationship with fondness on an anniversary, for example, or simply to keep in mind our grocery list when heading to the store. For our Hebrew brethren, however, to *remember* meant something far greater.

For the Jewish people, to remember meant to be rejoined to, almost to become one (member) with again. The Jews viewed remembering in a less temporal and more spiritual way, as if time almost stood still. It's for this reason, in part, that God repeatedly told the Jews of the Old Testament to "remember" his works. To reenact the Passover annually, for example, or to remember the revelation given them atop Mt. Sinai when moving forward in faith or walking in circles in the wilderness.

God understands how fickle we can be. This is, I think, one of the reasons for his constant admonition to remember. He wants us not only to recall, but to prayerfully re-engage, re-encounter, and re-immerse ourselves in the moments when he has revealed his love and faithfulness to us. This is the purpose not only of signs like wedding rings and sacramentals like holy water, but of the sacraments. This is why Jesus bid us to "do this in remembrance" and commanded us to do so every week in the Mass. God *knew* what we needed before we even asked for it. We need to be in his divine presence during the joys and the struggles of life, to offer thanks, or to seek healing, or to receive his love as Dismas did.

The miracle of Good Friday is that God didn't call on a miracle. He mounted that cross and took our place. We sinned and he was punished. We ran up the bill yet he arrived and paid the debt we couldn't pay. We cannot and must not ever forget who saved whom and who invites whom to abide in him. For a grape to offer its blood to make wine, it must first stay connected to the water of the vine. Likewise, for us to bear fruit throughout the season of life—even the droughts—we must be near enough to the Lord to hear his voice and remember his promise. It was as true for Dismas as it is for each of us as we advance toward the altar of sacrifice in our local church every Sunday.

From Head to Heart For Reflection

1. Choose one area of your life in which you know God is calling you to change. What specific steps can you take toward your goal? To whom can you be accountable as you begin this journey toward greater freedom?

2. When you remember various times in your life, do you tend to focus on where things went wrong or where they went right? How might prayer, counseling, the sacraments, or sharing with a trusted friend help you to remember the past in light of God's healing and merciful love for you?

A STEP BEYOND

Everyone has a cross to bear. Often, though, we are so overwhelmed by the weight of our own that we fail to notice the cross on the shoulders of those around us. Allow eye contact and intentional presence to be your form of prayer today or for the next few days. Make it a point to turn off your phone and screens. Make eye contact with everyone with whom you speak. Acknowledge Christ within them. Ask them questions. Validate their feelings. Offer hope for their situation. Affirm their goodness and beauty. See Christ, as Dismas did, as Savior even when others fail to do the same.

PRAYER

Lord Jesus, when I feel forgotten or abandoned, alone or afraid, in despair or in pain, bring me back to the foot of your cross. Through your perfect sacrifice please give me the perspective I need when I am spiritually shortsighted. Please reorient my heart to yours and help me to remember that you are always with me and within me, to help me bear any crosses that come my way. Amen.

A Personal Message from Mark Hart

7

Encountering Jesus Calls You to Greatness

CHRIST AND YOU

> You formed my inmost being;
> you knit me in my mother's womb.
> (Psalm 139:13, NABRE)

Somewhere in your home there are probably baby pictures. They might exist in photo albums or, worse yet, framed and on a shelf, waiting for all to see and goodheartedly mock during the next family gathering. There you are, diaper-clad, rolls of baby fat, and a future full of hope.

Those pictures do tell a story about you, however, and about your earthly beginnings. There might even be ultrasound pictures in an album somewhere, lest you forget that your life began nine months before you exited the womb. You had a beginning. God knit you in your mother's womb, as we are told in Scripture (see Psalm 139:13-16). He had a design for you and a purpose for you from the beginning (see Jeremiah 1:4-8), and that plan is for you to do good works (see Ephesians 2:10).

The point is that God was there from the beginning. You were his creation, made in his own image (see Genesis 1:27). Those pictures of you in the hospital celebrate your *natural* birth. Turn a couple of pages in that baby album, however, and you'll likely see another "birthday," the one on which God made you his own child through the *supernatural birth* at your Baptism.

JUST LIKE JESUS

The Gospel of Mark doesn't tell us anything about Jesus' childhood or earthly beginnings. The Gospels of Matthew and Luke consider the infancy of Jesus, but Mark begins with an already adult Jesus heading to the River Jordan.

Jesus wanted to be baptized, though he didn't need it. He did it to offer us an example, a living witness of what *we* need in order to live as a child of God.

What Mark describes in three verses is striking:

> In those days Jesus came from Nazareth of Galilee and was baptized by John in the Jordan. And when he came up out of the water, immediately he saw the heavens opened and the Spirit descending upon him like a dove;

and a voice came from heaven, "Thou art my beloved Son; with thee I am well pleased." (Mark 1:9-11)

This scene marks the first time God the Father speaks in the Gospels, which is noteworthy. The Father's words are important not only for Jesus to know but for us to hear. Jesus is God's Son, a fact God the Father makes clear here with his own voice. Can you imagine what that sounded like? God is pleased with Jesus—not that this was a news flash. Right now you might be thinking, "Of course he's proud, how could he not be? Jesus is the perfect kid, literally."

Remember, though, that Jesus hadn't done anything in public ministry yet. God's love of Jesus was not based on his perfection or his performance but on his person. The Father's love for his Son wasn't based on Jesus' resume; it was rooted in their relationship.

I've witnessed these three little verses reduce grown men to sobbing wrecks during retreats or parish missions. It's far easier for us to believe God loves Jesus than it is to believe that God truly, unconditionally, and eternally loves *us*—that he is in a relationship with each of us.

The key to this relationship is prayer. We mustn't make the mistake of thinking that prayer is something that merely helps or props up our relationship with God. Prayer is *essential* to our relationship with God! Without prayer, the relationship threatens to fade away even though God is always there, ready for us to rekindle our union with him.

Here's what I've found in my life: when it's most difficult to pray, that's a sign I really need to pray. When things haven't panned out the way I hoped they would, when sickness sets in, when financial stress becomes overwhelming, when marriages end, when family members move away (physically or emotionally)—that's when we need to reposition ourselves, knees to the floor, and refocus our eyes on the Lord. If we can do this in a church, before the Eucharist, all the better.

I'd like to ask you to pray with me now. Find a quiet space, and create some room for God to breathe and for you to exhale. Once you do, pray this prayer slowly.

He's Always There for You

Come, Holy Spirit.
Come, Holy Spirit.
Come, Holy Spirit.

Holy Spirit, come and fill this place.
Holy Spirit, come and be with me now.
Holy Spirit, come and dwell within me.

Holy Spirit, I give you permission to work in my life.
Holy Spirit, I give you permission to reveal my shame.
Holy Spirit, I give you permission to love me.

Come, Holy Spirit, dwell within my heart.
Come, Holy Spirit, shake my soul.
Come, Holy Spirit, reveal to me all you wish to show me this day.

Now picture yourself sitting alone in a chapel. Perhaps it's an Adoration chapel at your local parish or a side chapel in your childhood church. Place yourself within it. Take a minute to take in the artwork. Note the windows, the icons, the type of floor, the architecture, the colors and shapes that surround you. Feel the seat beneath you—is it a padded chair or a hardened pew?

Now focus on the tabernacle. Pay attention to its detail, its imagery, and design. Note the subtle but constant flicker of the red candle, the constant yet soft reminder of God's enduring presence among us (see Matthew 1:23, 28:20).

Take in the silence in the chapel. Whenever you feel yourself distracted by exterior noises or interior thoughts, just pray, "Come, Holy Spirit" until the distractions dissipate.

Now, a door opens to the chapel and someone enters. Don't turn to look; stay locked on the tabernacle. You hear footsteps moving down the aisle but you're focused. You hear the steps stop but you don't look away; your eyes are fixed on the Lord in his earthly dwelling.

The person who entered chooses to sit in your row, right beside you. But you, focused as you are, keep your eyes straight ahead until—suddenly—you realize that Christ the Lord is seated beside you.

Experience the Lord's presence. Sense him near you. This is your moment. This is your chance to speak. Trust him. Pour out your heart. What is it you most desperately want to ask or tell the Lord right now?

How would you start?
"Why, Lord, did you . . ."
"Why, Jesus, didn't you . . ."
"How could you . . ."
"Can you still . . ."

Whatever is in your heart, whatever you've said a thousand times before or whatever you've never had the courage to utter aloud, now is your chance. If you want to scream, go ahead—he can take it. If you need to vent, proceed. If you have questions, ask them. If you are overwhelmed to the point that you cannot speak, the Lord is fine with that, too.

If it helps to journal your thoughts, do so. If you need to put down your journal or this book and spend time in silence, go ahead. Allow the Spirit to lead you. Trust in his guidance and mercy.

Once you've had your chance to speak, focus on Christ once again. Really draw near to him. Lean into his grace; Jesus has something he wants to say to you. Let him speak. What would the Lord say to you?

Perhaps it might begin:

"My child, I've never left you . . ."
"Would I ever abandon you?"
"I died for you . . ."
"I've forgiven that sin . . . I've forgiven you . . ."
"This is not the life I desire for you . . ."
"I want to give you more . . ."
"Will you stop running?"

"Will you let me love you completely?"

What is the Lord saying to your heart, right now?

Is the Lord condemning you or is he inviting you to something greater, something deeper, something higher?

Sit with him, fix your eyes on him. Let him have the last word.

After a few moments, the Lord rises from the seat beside you. Do you sense that tug in your heart? Do you feel that pull in your chest, hoping he won't leave? Listen to his promise to be with you always. Now return your focus to the tabernacle. Zoom in on the red sanctuary candle's flicker. Close your eyes and focus on the moment.

God is with you, now and always, seen or unseen, felt or not felt. The Lord is always at your side.

Ever Forward

Have you heard God calling you to make some changes across any of these pages? Has the Spirit taken you back to an encounter with God from your past or, possibly, revealed a way God has been trying to get your attention in the present? What now?

Your life is your story and every good story—from both the greatest times in history and the darkest—has one thing in common: it produces the greatest heroes. Your story is still being written and the world needs that story. The world needs the person God created you to be.

Even if everyone else is against you, you still have Christ. He is available to you every second of every day. He is speaking to you in his word. He is present to you in his Church. He is available to you at every Mass. He promised, "I am with you always, until the end of the age" (Matthew 28:20). You are never alone. A good Father could never abandon his child. The Father has never had to give you a second look because he has never once taken his eyes off of you.

The Lord has counted "even the hairs of your head" (Matthew 10:30). He has "graven you on the palms of [his] hands" (Isaiah 49:16). He "will wipe away every tear" (Revelation 21:4). He delights in you; he sings over you (see Zephaniah 3:17). He died for you, rose for you, and abides in you (see John 15:4).

If you believe that the Holy Spirit dwells within you—as Christ promises—then you have no reason to doubt or underestimate your power. It's time to pour out some heroism on a world desperately in need of it. Allow the Holy Spirit to unleash the greatness of your soul.

Prayer

Lord God, thank you for the gift of your Church. Thank you for the opportunity to experience you not only in your word but in your Sacrament. Grant me the eyes of faith to see your true presence before me. Give me the grace to seek you often in your tabernacle and even more frequently at your altar. Fill me with your divine life here on earth as you lead me to a new life with you in heaven. Amen.

A Personal Message from Mark Hart

The Word Among Us publishes a monthly devotional magazine, books, Bible studies, and pamphlets that help Catholics grow in their faith.

To learn more about who we are and what we publish, visit www.wau.org. There you will find a variety of Catholic resources that will help you grow in your faith.

Your review makes a difference! If you enjoyed this book, please consider sharing your review on Amazon using the QR code below.

Embrace His Word
Listen to God . . .

www.wau.org